The Art of Book Writing

SHARI W. QUINN

To Sharia, Ruffus "Pop" & Malik

You will forever my babies. Keep reaching for the stars
and all your dreams will come true!

CONTENTS

ACKNOWLEDGMENTS

Thank you to everyone whom has encouraged and supported me during
this project; my dear friends, Karen Stratton, Angelica Morris, Heather
Rooney and Niskayuna Town Library. Thanks for all your support and
encouragement throughout this project.
You're such a blessing and I'm glad to call you friend.

Prelude

Everyone has a story to tell and many people have the dream of writing a book. Sitting down to write the book or even knowing how to get started can be a daunting task. Over the past couple of years, I have met many people whom shared their dream of writing and publishing a book or in some cases, many have shared their struggle of completing their book writing project after many years of writing.

To date, I have successfully completed and published three books: a best-selling fiction suspense novel, a how-to marketing book for authors, and a cookbook. I have also had the opportunity to facilitate many high-demand workshops on how to write a book and consulted many aspiring authors on achieving their dream. This how-to book will provide you with the elements of successful book writing, staying on task and completing your project in a reasonable amount of time.

By following these easy steps outlined in this book, you will be well on your way to achieving your dream of writing and publishing your book.

Let's get started.

Getting Started

Generally, beginning writers make the common mistake in thinking the first step in the book writing process is to just start writing. Before we begin actually writing the book, there are several critical steps proceeding that part of the process. Here's what you want to do first:

1. Set a Specific Goal and Deadline
Think about a realistic time frame of when you would like to complete your book writing book and when you would like the book to be on the book store shelves. Consider all the elements and activities you currently have going on in your life such as work, school, hobbies, children, children's sports activities and how much time you will have to commit to writing in order to

achieve the task. Set the goal, mark it on your calendar and write daily to meet your deadline.

2. Minimize Distractions

Now that you have determined your deadline, it's time to focus on the project. As a result, it's important to minimize your distractions. This may include not watching television, turning off or silencing your cellphone during your dedicated writing schedule, deactivating your social media pages, and minimize routine outings with friends and family during this time. The key is to stay focused on your project, you can return to the things you've eliminated once the project is complete or when you have reached a specific goal of the book project. Whatever you do, keep all distractions to a minimum or completely eliminate them, if possible.

3. Find a Dedicated Space

Only you know the best writing space for you. Perhaps it's your home office, a corner in your bedroom, the dinner table or public library. Wherever it is, make it a comfortable and quiet space for you to retreat and enter into your writing zone. The area should be clear of noise, disruptions and clutter. This is where you will spend majority, if not all, of your time writing. Make it your own dedicated space.

4. Be Consistent

The key to writing and completing your book is consistency. It's very easy to get distracted and thrown off course. At this point, nothing should get in your way. Determine the best time of day for you to write based on your schedule, and develop a plan for your writing routine that you can realistically stick to. Write in on your calendar, schedule your writing time and be consistent with your schedule. When I wrote my first novel, I viewed it as a part-time job. I wrote every day from 6pm to midnight. I gave myself a 30-minute dinner break to make a quick meal for my son, and returned to writing immediately after the 30-minute break. Once I entered my zone, it was always difficult to stop writing but I would end writing at mid-might or shortly after. Following the consistent schedule, I was able to finish writing the book in a little over 90 days.

5. Write Every Day

This is part of the consistency: writing every single day. At a minimum, you should 1,000 words per day. This will not only help you maintain consistency but help you development as a writer. If you're writing a novel, you should want to write a least 5-10 pages or a chapter per day. Set a word or page count goal for yourself.

It'll help you stay on task and on schedule of meeting your deadline.

<u>Average word count</u>:

10,000 words – a pamphlet/booklet

20,000 words - a short print book or eBook

40,000 – 50,000 words – nonfiction book

60,000 – 70,000 words – a longer nonfiction

80,000 – 100,000 words – typical fiction book

If for any reason you're not writing, you should be working on something related to your project. Whether its research, interviewing subjects or brainstorming, you should consistently be working on your project during the allotted time schedule.

6. <u>Write an Author's Bio</u>

Typically writers think of writing their biography last but it's actually one of the beginning steps of writing your book. As you begin writing and talking about your project, you'll want to begin marketing your book as well. You should have your biography prepared and on hand to share for media and publicity purposes. If you plan to create a website for your book, which you should it now and add your bio to your website as well to inform readers and the public of who you are, your credentials and inspiration of writing this book.

7. <u>Back Up Your Work</u>

This is probably one of the most important aspects of writing: backing up your work. My doctoral professor often reminded us during our dissertation writing to "back up your back up". You should have a USB, a cloud account and an email address to send your work to yourself. Save each version and each new chapter to your USB and Cloud account, email to yourself and repeat. The worst thing you can do is lose your work. If you happen to lose your work, you will become discouraged, want to throw it the towel and not start over so do yourself a favor in backing up your work. Saving in three different areas sounds tedious but it'll save you the head-ache. Certainly do not rely on saving only to your USB because with Murphy's Law, "anything that can go wrong, will". You could lose your USB, it could also get damaged or encrypted so again, save it to your Cloud account as well.

8. <u>A Notebook</u>

You should have at least two-to-three notebooks readily available to jot down your thoughts and ideas. Keep a notebook in the car, on your nightstand, and in your purse or briefcase. As writers, we are always thinking and coming up with new ideas to add to our story, jot it down and do not rely on memory. Chances are you will forget it later. All ideas are good ideas regardless if you use them or not. Go out and get yourself notebooks or journals today.

9. Thesaurus

For obvious reasons, you'll want to have a thesaurus on hand. You'll want to be descriptive in your writing and not be repetitive in using the same words. Using a thesaurus and keeping in handy, will help you add color, dimension to your story and increase the tone of your language.

10. 3-Ring Binder

When you begin the writing process, you'll save and print each chapter separately. Don't worry about organizing the structure of your book by chapters now, you'll complete this once you finish the entire project. For now, print each chapter and insert into your binder using number divider tabs. Don't worry about titling the chapters in the beginning, it'll come to you when you're finished writing the story.

You will later discover when you're completely finished with writing, what you thought was your Chapter 3 may end up as your Chapter 12. Likewise, Chapter 19 may very well become Chapter 1. So again, for now, save, print and put in your binder. Organize the chapters later. Thus, you don't have to write in order of your outline because you'll soon find out, it'll change.

Building a House Method

Building your story is very similar to building a home. Every home is built with a strong foundation and structure, and built in phases. Likewise, your story should be built on a solid foundation which is your outline. In my "How to Write a Book" workshops, I teach my clients to build their story using the "Building a House Method".

1. Write a One Sentence Summary

2. Expand to a One Paragraph Summary (approximately 5 sentences)

3. Set up a 3-Act Structure (3 Disasters/Conflicts)

4. Back Cover (Should Only Summarize ¼ of the Story)

5. Summary of Characters

6. Book Outline

7. Book Structure

8. Write the Story

9. Begin and End with a Bang!

If you're writing an average length book, it will be anywhere from 100-400 pages. We will explore each of these elements throughout the book.

Concept of Book

Defining the concept of your book will help you articulate the purpose and vision of book. Think about why you're writing this book, what you're trying to achieve and the message. This will help give you a clear direction and aide you in staying on task to achieve the purpose of the book. In forming the concept, you should:

1. Write a one-sentence summary

2. Write a one-paragraph summary

3. Determine Genre, Language and Time Period

4. Write your book Outline

5. Write your Summary of Characters

A one sentence summary about the book will also become your 15-second elevator pitch to avoid rambling when someone asks you about your book. For example, my one sentence summary about my book is, "It's a suspense fiction novel about the betrayal of friendships that lead to a twisting murder plot". It's very simple, concise and to the point but enough to leave the prospective reader intrigued to purchase and read the book. You don't want to ramble on and on, and on about your book; and you certainly don't want to give the entire story away. Give potential readers just enough to have a good idea of what the plot or book is about, and enough to make them want to buy your book.

The one-paragraph summary is for your eyes only. It'll guide you in the direction of your book with the plot of the story, the characters, the conflict, climax and conclusion of the book. You'll type this out, keep it handy in your binder and refer to it often to ensure you're including these elements in your book and fulfilling its purpose. For an example of a one-paragraph summary, here's what I used for my fiction novel:

Disloyalty is an intense 222-page suspense novel about lust, betrayal, and friendships gone wrong. The betrayer forms a surprising and betraying love affair with the man her best friend is dating which quickly spirals into an alleged murder-for-hire plot. Feeling defeated by repeated flawed plans to murder their wealthy friend, they race to desperate measures before running out of time. Since the once trusted best friends are now rivals, it's the perfect opportunity for other seemingly clever and deceptive individuals to maximize the distraction, and rush to the finish line while all eyes are on the betrayer. Loyalty, authenticity and friendships are challenged, and the core of characters exposed. Bizarre events validates no one can be trusted, everyone is in question, and the allegiance to greed is unyielding. This fast-paced dark, thriller reveals jaw-dropping surprises and unthinkable secrets with every turn of the page. Nail-biting discoveries of unsuspecting accomplices and decoys will shock you.

My one paragraph summary was very helpful as it kept me on task of the purpose of the book. It later became the back cover of my book and book summary for readers to determine if they wanted to purchase and read the book.

In determining the language of your story, consider if you're going to tell the story in first person or third person. If you're writing in first person, you're going to make sure you, as the main character, are present throughout the book to tell the story. If in third person, you'll use pronouns such as he, she, they; and write as the narrator of the story. It's common to switch back and forth from first to third person so select one language for consistency.

Decide the time period of your story: present day, past tense, modern day, 50-years ago, medieval or a historical period. This is a critical element of writing because you'll want to make sure the details and descriptions of your details match the time period or era of what you are writing. For example, if your setting is the 1950's in the South, you're more likely to write about a relevant car in that time period such as a classic 1957 light blue, hardtop convertible Chevy with large headlights versus a 2016 sporty red Maserati. Be sure to do your research when describing details during specific time periods for accuracy and believability, this applies to clothing articles as well.

We'll discuss writing your book outline and summary of characters shortly.

Creating Your Outline

As we learned in elementary school, the most important aspect of writing a story is drafting an outline. Do not skip this part. It's probably the most grueling but you will thank yourself later as it'll connect all the dots to your book.

When creating your outline, you can either use an Excel spreadsheet, create a template in Word or draw a chart on a blank sheet of paper. Regardless of which you decide, create a chart with six (6) columns down and start with 10 rows across. This will increase or decrease depending on how many chapters you have.

Your columns across should read as follows:

1. Scene – What is happening in this scene or chapter?

2. POV (Point of View) – From whose point of view are you telling the story? Who is telling the story in this scene or chapter?

3. Characters – Which characters are present in this chapter or scene?

4. Goal – What is the goal of the chapter? Make sure it meets and connects to the overall goal of the book which you identified earlier in your purpose statement.

5. Details – What is happening in this chapters? What are the main points?

6. Conflict – What is the conflict in this scene? What occurs that prevents the goal of the character being achieved?

Once you've prepared your outline, you're ready to begin your story .... which is almost finished now that you have your outline. This is the core of your book.

Your scenes will later become your chapters. Don't worry about organizing your chapters now. Again, after you complete each scene or chapter, print and store in your binder to organize the order of the chapters later.

Summary of Characters

The *Summary of Characters* is for your eyes only and is a guide for you as you are creating your characters. As you are creatively writing your story and creating character development, it will be difficult for you to remember every detail about the characters or how you identified them in your story. As I have mentioned several times, do not rely on your memory. When I wrote about the detailed characteristics of the antagonist in one chapter and wrote about them in subsequent chapters, I couldn't recall the age I gave them or what part of town I fictionally created as their residence or other important characteristics. The *Summary of Characters* was a helpful point of reference to maintain consistency in the story and character.

This reference guide is just that, a guide for you for character development and consistency throughout your chapters. It'll also help you to bring your characters to life for your readers.

To create your Summary of Characters, create in a Word Document or Excel Spreadsheet. You will continually add to this as you develop their character:

- List Every Character
- Main Characters
- Secondary Characters
- Be very descriptive

In the Summary include:

- Character's Name
- Character's Storyline (one paragraph)
- Motivation (Abstractly)
- Their goal (Concretely)
- Conflict (What prevents them from reaching their objective?)
- Epiphany (What will they learn? How will they change?)

Here's an example of a Character Summary, written as a Word document:

Caleb McElroy, 46, an attractive, tall, slim man; very desirable by the ladies, army veteran with a dishonorable discharge. He's an airline baggage handler for South Jet Airlines and has been on the job nine-years. He's also a bootlegger, and seller of DVD movies and music CD's out his car. Caleb briefly dated Laila for two years. He is very selfish, conniving and manipulative but presents himself as a charismatic, compassionate and respectful. He adores nice things, drives three luxury cars and owns a 19-ft Sea Ray boat, all gifted by his live-in terminal-ill Canadian roommate, Ava. As most opportunists, he's always looking to see how he can benefit from someone else. During his relationship with Laila, he discovers her best friend, Gina of 25-years, is the Executor and Trustee of her Last Will and Testament, and charms Gina into a steamy sexual relationship although he has no romantic interest with her. During his six-month affair with Gina, he plots a murder-for-hire to kill Laila unbeknownst to Gina. His plan is to kill Laila so he can enjoy and share the wealth of the $500,000 life insurance money entrusted to Gina to manage for Laila's minor 13-year old child, Zion.

All the while, Caleb lives with a Canadian woman, Ava, who is dying from lung cancer. Ava believes she's been in a 9-year relationship with Caleb, but he has no romantic interest in her either but only in his inheritance of her life $300,000 insurance policy and the 5,500 sq. ft. mortgage-free rural home they share on 7.5 acres. He forged a father-son relationship with Ava's son, Chase, who received a large settlement allowing the son to purchase the home for his mother, which Caleb muscled her into listing his name in the deed. Chase has since graduated high school and is serving as an Officer in the United Stated Navy, stated in Germany. He is currently planning a wedding and with his fiancée with no intention of returning back to the home he purchased for his mother. Therefore, should Ava die, Caleb will theoretically take ownership of the home since Chase has no plan on returning.

With two women potentially dead, Caleb stands to gain nearly a million dollars but he only has until the stroke of midnight of New Year's Eve before the policy expires.

Print your Summary of Characters and insert it into

the inside pocket of your 3-ring binder for easy reference.

This is one of the most important aspects of developing

your character and you will refer to this summary often. I found myself writing all over printed sheet as I added more details of the each character. Again, this is a tool for you and will not be printed in your story. As mentioned, do not rely on your memory.

When you are writing about your characters, introduce them to your readers and be descriptive throughout your writing. For example, if they flick their cigarette when they smoke, describe what that looks like; describe how they walk with a limp or their heavy Southern accent when they talk.

Book Anatomy

1. Half Title Page

2. Title Page

    On the title page, you'll simply just have the title of the book in the middle of the page along with your name as the author at the bottom. Leave plenty of room between the title and your name, as this will also become your signature page during book signings. Speaking of the signature page, write down a few inscriptions of what you'd like to write when signing your book: "Best wishes", "Thank you for your support", "Hope you enjoy the book", etc.

When autographing the book, always ask the person to spell their name, even if they have a common name such as Michelle since some people may spell it with one L. You may feel like you're offending them by asking but it's more offensive and even embarrassing for your supporter tell you that you have misspelled their name. Save yourself the trouble and embarrassment, and ask. Always keep a few Sharpie's on hand to sign books.

3. Copyright Page

This is also known as the legal page.

4. Dedication Page

You do not have to title this the Dedication. Once you begin with "This book is dedicated to ..., your readers will know it's the dedication page. Just begin with whom you're dedicating to.

5. Acknowledgments (Optional)

These are the people that have supported you, helped you or motivated you along with journey of your book writing, and you'd like to give them a special thank you or acknowledgement of their support. You are not limited to the number of people to thank but you should keep this limited to one page.

6. Table of Contents

Under the table of contents, list each chapter along with the Preface and Acknowledgements. The book should end with the About Author page. Your completed bio will come in handy here. Each chapter should be referenced with the accurate corresponding page number. Be sure your publisher, editor or interior designer has properly formatted your Table of Contents with the correct page numbers. This could be a major mishap if the book is printed with incorrect page numbers after you've made edits and the pages were not adjusted.

7. The Book!

Elements of Storytelling

When writing your story, it is critical to be descriptive and write three-dimensionally. Show, not tell. Instead of storytelling, I refer to is as Show-telling. Your thesaurus will come in handy throughout your book to help you champion this aspect of writing. Be sure to add color and character to your story. Your readers should feel as if they are physically present in the story. If the scene in your story has a rich aroma of fresh roasted, French vanilla coffee in the air, your reader should be able to imagine the smell of the coffee.

Since you are not writing a film to give your audience a visual, you will have to show your readers the details of every moment. It is your responsibility to make sure you provide enough descriptive details and a paint a vivid picture for them. Carry your readers with you. Provide specifics and they will stay will you to the end. Of course, add conflict, a ticking-clock to create suspense or intrigue.

Helpful tips when writing:

- Avoid starting with weather

- Start your story with a bang. You only have the first paragraph to capture and keep their reader's attention.

- Never use a verb other than "said" to carry dialogue (or use sparingly)

- Keep exclamation points under control (no more than 2-3 per 100,000 words)

- Never use the word "suddenly" (or use sparingly)

- Use regional dialect sparingly

- Leave out the part that readers tend to skip. If it's boring to you, it'll be boring to your readers.

- Use transitions

- Be very descriptive – bring the story to life

Editing

Most authors wait until they have completed the book to begin editing the project. I would strongly encourage you to edit after each completed chapter before proceeding to the next. Undoubtedly, you will be eager to begin writing the next chapter. However, if you edit as you go along you will reduce the work in half and catch errors or weaknesses early on. This will cut down your editing time in the end, significantly reduce your editing costs since Editors charge by the hour and it will help strengthen your storyline and tone as you continue to write your book.

Helpful editing tips:

- Read out loud to yourself (at least 3x)

- Use pencil – pens bleed through printed paper

- Use a thesaurus

- Tighten up your story

- Consistency in Language & Timing

- Hire an Experienced Book Editor (for structure editing)

- Avoid peculiar and jazzy font types (Comic, Sans, Times Roman)

- Use a Reader-friendly Font (Serif, Baskerville, Garamond, Horley Old Style)

Publishing

__Now Signing New and Experienced Authors__

Hopefully, you have signed a book deal with a major book publishing company. However, the chances of that are very slim.

Shari Quinn Publishing provides premier book publishing services to aspiring authors. We provide the experience and the know-how of book publishing in this competitive and complicated climate. We will assist you with strategically marketing and branding your book for maximum exposure to increase sales and readers.

Book Publishing Services:

- Set-up
- Book formatting to Trim Size (5x8 or 6x9)
- Publishing
- E-book conversation
- ISBN
- Bar Code
- Copyright
- Proof of your book
- Printing

A la Carte Services:

- Press releases
- Advertising
- Book launch
- Schedule book signing
- Book trailer
- Consultation
- Editing

Rates & Royalties

- Authors keeps rights to their book
- Quarterly royalties

Submission requirements

- First 2 chapters
- Book Synopsis or Proposal (1 Page)
- Book Title
- Page and Word Count

If you have been wanting to write a book, struggled with getting your book published or simply do not know how to get started, contact shari@shariquinn.com or for a complimentary consultation or go to shariquinn.com for more information.

About the Author

Shari W. Quinn, a native of Albany, New York, is the best-selling author of *Disloyalty*, *42 Strategies to Market Your Book* and the cookbook *Taste!* She is also NBC's Albany affiliate, WNYT News Channel 13's *Today's Woman*. After living in suburban Atlanta for eight years, she relocated back to New York's Capital Region. She is a leader in education, a college instructor, and has been in the higher education industry for more than 16 years. She has served as a guest speaker in over 75 high schools throughout New York State.

She earned her Master's degree in Business Administration (MBA) with a concentration in Marketing from the University of Phoenix in Atlanta; a Bachelor's in Marketing and Management from Siena College in Loudonville, New York; and an Associate's degree in Liberal Arts from Hudson Valley Community College in Troy, New York. She has completed more than two years toward her Doctor of Education (Ed.D.) degree in Educational Leadership, and is currently pursuing her doctoral degree with Northeastern University in Boston.

She is the proud mother of three adult children, Sharia, Ruffus "Pop" IV, and Malik; has two beautiful grandchildren, Anthony Jr., and DeShari'ay; and lives in upstate New York.